THE MEANING OF *Life*

GERALD G. FRIERSON

Copyright © 2020 by Gerald G. Frierson.

ISBN   978-1-970160-93-2 Ebook
ISBN   978-1-970160-94-9 Paperback

All rights reserved. No part of this publication may be reproduced, distributed, or transmitted in any form or by any means, including photocopying, recording, or other electronic or mechanical methods without the prior written permission of the publisher. For permission requests, solicit the publisher via the address below through mail or email with the subject line "Attention: Publication Permission".

The EC Publishing LLC books may be ordered
through booksellers or by contacting:

EC Publishing LLC
116 South Magnolia Ave.
Suite 3, Unit F
Ocala, FL 34471, USA
Direct Line: +1 (352) 644-6538
Fax: +1 (800) 483-1813
http://www.ecpublishingllc.com/

Ordering Information:
Quantity sales. Special discounts are available on quantity purchases by corporations, associations, and others. For details, contact the publisher at the address above.

Printed in the United States of America

ABOUT THE AUTHOR/BOOK

Gerald G. Frierson has a Bachelor of Arts degree in criminal justice from Temple University. He also, graduated from the PJA paralegal school. It is during this education that he developed his unique and clever writing style. This is a life's work for Mr. Frierson and his first book. Also, Mr. Frierson has started his own Life Coaching company which is based largely on the book and is called G FRIERSON MARKETING INC.

Life teaches us that we have many choices or no choice at all. We can choose to believe in GOD or not to believe in GOD. You can choose to believe in yourself or not to believe in yourself. You can believe in something or you can believe in nothing. But we should always choose life over death. If

Gerald G. Frierson

life has no meaning then there is really no reason to live. We should always try and live life to the fullest. GOD is the reason why we live but how we live is totally up to us. "THE MEANING OF LIFE" is a true story, and not necessarily because it's true but because of what it teaches you about life. Life's about choices and what this book does is help you to make the right choices for you, good or bad, right or wrong. Ultimately, you will have to make and take responsibility for your own decisions in life. What this book does is help you navigate your way through your choices and through life. And remember your decisions not only affect you but everyone around you. How can you truly be happy if everyone around you is unhappy? The ultimate goal of "THE MEANING OF LIFE" is to help everyone who reads it discover his or her purpose in life. Congratulations! You have just discovered "THE MEANING OF LIFE" now please tell all your friends and loved ones. "Thank You" and Enjoy!

GERALD G. FRIERSON

AN INTRODUTION TO: "THE MEANING OF LIFE"

Life teaches us that we have many choices or no choice at all. We can choose to believe in GOD or not to believe in GOD. You can choose to believe in yourself or not to believe in yourself. You can believe in something or you can believe in nothing. But we should always choose life over death. If life has no meaning, then there is really no reason to live. We should always try and live life to the fullest. GOD is the reason why we live but how we live is totally up to us. But the most important thing is not where we came from but where we are going, both, as individuals and as a people. Even if you do not believe in GOD, we should still hold ourselves accountable for the things we do as a civilized society. Life must not be viewed as a competition. Everyone deserves to be happy and live a good life. Everyone should win and there should be no losers in the game of life. We all have the right to the necessities of life- proper health care, food, shelter, clothing, education, and the opportunity to participate in life. Why can't we all be happy? Even the 12th man on an NBA basketball team gets a ring if the team wins the championship although he never plays in the games. He is still happy because he gets a chance to participate in practice to prepare his team for the games. And although he is the 12th man he is probably still a millionaire and that is why everyone wants to be on the team. In addition, the fans of that team get to participate by cheering for and supporting the team. In the game of life, we should all be given an opportunity to be on the team no matter what your skill level is. And in the game of life all the teams should be successful. But GOD will not have favor on you because of the type of job you have, how much money you make, how many degrees you have, the type house you live in or type of car you drive. All GOD cares about is the strength of your spirit and your ability to follow it and Him unconditionally. Although, GOD will always allow you to claim these things, (just like He allows you to claim Salvation), because in fact He owns it all. But as a side note: while Salvation is free, degrees, jobs, houses, and cars are not; so, although you can claim them, you must work to get them and live within your means. Therefore, GOD is constantly trying to provide us with opportunities to be successful. All we must do is recognize and take advantage of them. In order to make the most of these opportunities we must teach each other and learn to work together. Education is the key. It is not enough that we just invest money, jobs, time, and resources. We must teach each other how to combine and use these resources for the betterment of society. Everyone can teach, if only about themselves and everyone is different. We must embrace these differences in order to find the best solutions to life's problems. All the best teachers provide you with all the questions, all the answers and then help you match them up. Life teaches us that we have many choices or no choice at all. But we should always choose life over death. I would hope that most people believe that this choice is no choice at all. Since most us would choose life; we should find ways to live a rewarding, happy and fulfilled life. This book was written to help you do just that. "THE MEANING OF LIFE" is a true story, and not necessarily because it is true but because of what it teaches you about life. Life's about choices and what this book does is help you to make the right choices for you, good or bad, right or wrong. Ultimately, you will have to make and take responsibility for your own decisions in life. What this book does is help you navigate your way through your choices and through life. And remember your decisions not only affect you but everyone around you. How can you truly be happy if everyone around you is unhappy? The ultimate goal of "THE MEANING OF LIFE" is to help everyone who reads it discover his or her purpose in life. Congratulations! You have just discovered "THE MEANING OF LIFE" now please tell all your friends and loved ones. "Thank You" and Enjoy!

GERALD G. FRIERSON

THE MEANING OF LIFE

PERFECT: to be without flaw.
HENCE, NO ONE IS PERFECT

Perfection, in and of itself, is not perfect unless it occurs strictly by chances and never by choices or by God for, He would or could never take a chance. Imperfectly Imperfect- the only way we can be perfect is to not be perfect all the time. In other words, perfection is the process of not being perfect all the time (time heals all wounds). Anything can be perfect until it is broken but not everything that is broken can be fixed. But sometimes in order to fix something we must first take it apart and start from the beginning. Beauty is in the eye of the beholder; in other words, no one can be perfect until everyone is imperfectly imperfect. God would call this Heaven! Before we can achieve this impossible fate, we must first learn to all work together because everyone's life can and will affect everyone else's life. We must first all go back to school and learn to teach each other. God never meant for us to be perfect just "imperfectly imperfect." Everyone can achieve this state but unfortunately everyone will not be willing to do the "Work". You must first learn to be a student before you can truly teach. Unfortunately, everyone will not be willing to listen. The only thing that is perfect is time and space, and GOD of course; and GOD is everything. The only thing that is absolutely perfect on Earth is Life and death. And in between these two states we must try to be "imperfectly imperfect". We all make mistakes so we all should learn to accept God's grace and mercy and stop making the same mistakes over and over again. At some point you would figure we would learn from our mistakes and just follow God's Will. God never meant to spoil our fun; he just wants us to do it his way. There is a time and a place for just about everything. None of us were worthy but through his grace and mercy he will accept you any way as long as you accept Him first. We just have to follow his word and be of good Faith. We must believe in him for he believes in us. Life is all about Sacrifice. In order for our lives to grow, prosper, blossom or bear fruit we must first make sacrifices. Life without sacrifices is barren (cannot bear fruit). Through sacrifice is the only way we can learn from our mistakes and follow gods will. Jesus made the ultimate sacrifice; he gave his life so that we might live. For that we should all be thankful and live our lives accordingly. That is the only way we can honestly say "Thank You."

Let Jesus know he did not die in vain and just say "Thank You" by our words and actions: for actions sometimes speak louder than words. Only God can be perfect all the time so we should just try and learn how to walk like Jesus for he was and still and always will be the only one who will ever live and die perfect. And finally, last, but definitely not least, we must always remember that God, Jesus, and Holy Ghost have no equals, never have and never will. Therefore, God can, only, and must answer only to Himself. But God made quiet an investment in the world and us so please do not let Him lose his entire investment. God will always work for his Children, but he will never volunteer because He will always expect Credit. God's only job is to serve and protect his investment. So, we should all show some appreciation and just say "Thank You", and hope He responds, "You're Welcome, job well done!"

THE PROOF

In "real life" one + one does *not* equal two. One + one "only" equal two if the two things do not "truly" combine. In real life one + one equals either one or three or sometimes more but "never" two. It only equals two if the two things do not truly combine. Let me explain, for example, if a man and a woman truly combine and have a baby together that would equal three. Mother + father + baby = three people or one family. Hence, three or one or more if the mother has more than one child. One + one only equals two if the 2 do not truly combine or are not compatible but not even then, really; because they would then either be <u>one</u> couple, <u>one</u> marriage, <u>one</u> family, or <u>one</u> relationship. It would only = 2 if the man or the woman leaves the relationship or the two were never a couple or were never compatible in the first place (and who wants that). They would then be two or more sets of one not two.

And as we all know the whole is always greater than the sum of its parts. So, by definition one + one cannot equal two. But as a side note, the two could remain friends, (but would not that be <u>one</u> relationship), fortunately we can never have too many friends just too many enemies. And our number one enemy is Satan. You see, science teaches us that the Universe is made up of all "energy" that can neither be created nor destroyed. Therefore, before there was anything there had to be one and that one had to be God. God is a spirit that is made up of 100% pure positive energy. The thing is, God did not just create the Universe He was the Universe. Satan is made up of 100% negative energy. What this means is that the two could never mix. God created the heavens and the earth with positive energy. And whenever you create something with positive energy there will always be the creation of negative energy (waste) that energy turned into Satan. We need negative energy so we can learn how to fight sickness and decease and to stay positive when we make our mistakes. Interestingly enough, when we combine positive energy with more positive energy it increases in size and scope. But when we combine negative energy with more negative energy it decreases in size and scope, but it becomes more volatile or unstable and therefore more dangerous. What we should learn from these facts is that we should try to maximize the good effects of positive energy while minimizing bad effects of negative energy. For positive energy creates life and negative energy destroys or breaks down life. We can do this in one of two ways; 1) by isolating the negative energy from any and all positive energy and it will eventually destroy itself; and/or 2) you can overwhelm the negative energy with enough positive energy so that it turns itself into positive energy. Let's take the example of a house fire (negative energy), if left unchecked (isolation) the fire could not only burn up that house it could burn up the entire block but if the fire is caught in time the house can be saved and built back-up to be better than the original (positive energy). Another example is a criminal who is sent to prison as punishment for his crime (negative energy) without any positive energy being injected in the situation. What invariably happens is that the criminal learns that society only respects him or her as criminal and not as a man or woman and ends up going back to prison. And finally, when a man and woman get married, the marriage becomes far greater than the sum of its parts- the man and the woman (positive energy). If this does not happen the marriage is much more likely to end up in divorce or become an unhappy marriage. This usually happens because the man or woman or both put their individual needs (parts) ahead of the needs of the marriage (whole). As a result, any outside or inside negative energy can easily break-up the marital bond. In other words, in order for the marriage to operate at its best the marriage must become greater than the sum of its parts and not two sets of one. What we should get out of these stories is that we can only serve one Master not two. God is either one (God almighty) or three – the Father, the Son, and Holy Spirit, never two. God and Satan are two sets of one not two. God is the only true Master and Satan is only a fake Master but sadly many follow him anyway. Do not get me wrong, on paper one + one does equal two but in "real life" it only equals either one or three or more but "never two."

BY: GERALD G. FRIERSON

THE MORAL OF THIS STORY

The moral of this story is: we should all try and learn how to do the things we do best and let God handle the rest. All we have to do is just follow our own God given Spirit and learn from our mistakes for your own Spirit will never lead you wrong. Adam and Eve did not die they just went back to school (they were god's first born). That is what happens when you try to outsmart God for; He always knows what is best. Job one was that of Parent (synonymous with teacher) and God was the first Parent. Why do not we just follow his lead. Yes, Adam and Eve were disobedient to God, but the mistake was not theirs it was Satan's. You see, God had a plan for him too but he (much like us) was unwilling to wait on the Lord. For all intents and purposes, Satan was like God's brother, Adam and Eve's uncle. So, it was not Adam and Eve's fault, Satan was a grown-up and he should have known better. God would *never* blame His kids. The forbidden fruit represented Adam and Eve's *sacrifice.* God understands better than anyone that in order for the *world* to not only survive but thrive we must all learn how to make sacrifices. No one is exempt, not even Himself- just ask Jesus. So, when Adam and Eve could not wait and ate the forbidden fruit, he knew He had to come up with another way to teach us how to learn how to make sacrifices; that is when sin was born. We must all learn to wait on the Lord. But God, fortunately, had a Plan and from that plan He has never wavered. You see, God was victim too, and we should learn that we should almost never blame the victim because they usually did not know they were putting themselves in harm's way. But ignorance is still no excuse, that's why education is so important and why we should never stop learning. Although, ignorance can still be blissful because somethings you just do not need to know. "Does anybody know what's in Chinese food?" …. "I know, I don't know anyone who does either, but I won't let that stop me from enjoying some Chinese food every once in a while. But let us not get crazy here, there's are still things on the menu that I would never try and that would be O.K. too." "Or how about this, I know we've all done somethings in our past that you would never ever want your mother and/or father, or spouse to ever find out about." But get this, I hope it was not captured on film because silence may be golden, and you do have a constitutional right to remain silent; but pictures and videos can speak volumes. I know we can all relate to that." Even God can relate to this too because everyone was giving him the silent treatment yet He has film on everyone so He knew everyone could use His help. God will help anyone, but He would never volunteer because He would never want to take responsibility for your life away from you, therefore, you must ask for His help. Frustrated to no end, God had all but given up on the world but thanks to Jesus that did not happen. Jesus made the ultimate sacrifice He gave up His life so that we might live. He knew none of us were worthy, yet He gave his life anyway. The world as we know it today would not exist if He had not died for our sins. For that we should all say a big "THANK YOU, JESUS." Now, the question we must ask ourselves is what sacrifice or sacrifices (short of death) are we willing to make so the Lord will come down and redeem you. Are you ready to even ask Him to forgive you for your sins and save you; for He will not volunteer. When the time comes to approach the gates of heaven will the lord be able to greet you by saying "YOUR WELCOME MY CHILD JOB WELL DONE! Or will he say "SORRY, BUT *YOU ARE TOO LATE.*" You do not want the later to happen to you so call him today because no one knows how much time we have left. Tomorrow is never promised to us because it may never come so live for today but plan for the future. Call on Him today so your prepared either way, why take a chance when you do not have too. God will always go out of his way to be fair because He wants everyone to make it into Heaven. In that regard, to Adam and Eve God would, first, like to say **"sorry," "it was my fault. But I believe you both now realize I did it on purpose because I had a plan and knew it was for the best."** You both can come home now. I have redeemed you both. You have learned your lessons well! Thank you, job well done! "The two of you have earned my respect. I look forward to seeing you both on Thanksgiving, we have a lot to catch up on." They would then reply: "awe, dad you don't have to apologize to us, we've always known, that is as soon as we stopped apologizing to each other. That is why you never heard us complain. In turn, we would both like to thank you for being a wonderful and loving father. And for that we say "Job well done" to you as well for we could not have done it without you. "Thanks for inviting us home for Thanksgiving, we would not miss it for nothing in the world. (as a side note: God never said Adam and Eve were husband and wife- they were teacher and student Eve was the teacher and Adam was the student. They just procreated to keep the Race going. That was their Job.)

Love Always:

Adam and Eve

Of course, the above two letters or conversations are fictional but whose to really say whether this or a similar conversation has or will ever take place. What we must first, as individuals and then as families determine if we have given God enough reason to invite us back home as well. In other words, have you given God enough reason to redeem you? Have you called on the Lord to redeem and save you? If you need God's help you must ask Him for it, he will not volunteer because He always expects credit. When God gives you a gift, (and life is pretty special) always remain humble because any gift He gives you He can always take back. So always remember to always say "THANK YOU" and show your appreciation and God will work for you always. Remember none of us were worthy we all fell short of God's glory. So, we should all learn how to accept God's grace and mercy because once you accomplish this you can live in the house of the Lord forever. If you agree with any this, you should call on Jesus this very moment for God will not wait forever. That is right start praying right this very second; from wherever you are reading this; do not wait! What harm could it do? All you need is to be in a position and a place where you can safely keep your eyes closed 15 to 20 minutes. Everyone can use a little quiet time anyway. Do not know how to pray? Then start off by telling Jesus just that and then just tell him what is on your mind. (no secret to it). Do not believe in God? Then I do not know how you got this far into this paper. But since you did, I have one question for you. What happens if you are wrong? 20 minutes is not going to kill you, but it could save your LIFE. Then read this paper again from start to finish and share it with someone you care about. "THANK YOU"

BY : GERALD G. FRIERSON

WHAT is God's Salvation?

This is a narration by God.

Everyone fell short of God's glory. That is right everybody failed (yes, him too)! This angered God the most, not one person trusted that he knew what He was doing. But because his son Jesus was willing (on his own) to die for our sins He decided to save us anyway. Why did salvation take so long? God was waiting on the grandkids, for He knew one of them would finally get it right. God knew before He could execute His plan of Salvation, He knew he needed at least one person to finally get it right or his plan would fail. He had to find at least one person who was smart enough and willing to wait on the Lord "unconditionally." God stopped speaking to us after His Son died on the Cross. Instead He speaks to or feeds our own individual God given spirit. This is why if you want to talk God you must go through Jesus and the Holy Spirit. But once you learn how to communicate with your own individual God given human spirit you can talk directly to God. Unfortunately, most people are not willing to listen or do the work. (as a side note: your spirit is the only part of you that truly belongs to God.) Everyone gets one of these spirits at birth but no teaches us how to use it. The key to Salvation is that you should never depend just on your own understanding. You must, first, consider all the relevant facts in your life and learn how to follow your own God given spirit unconditionally, for it will never lead you wrong. If, when, or once you learn how to follow your own human spirit unconditionally, you will be able to speak to God himself. If, when, or once you ever get to this point you should ask God not to keep you or to save you but to let you go. Because at this point you would have already known that you were saved, it was your birth rite its everybody's birth rite. All you or anyone had to do was claim it. This is truly the easiest way to salvation. Salvation was always meant to be challenging but not difficult. For once you get to the point where you ask God to let you go, He

The Meaning of Life

will then complete you by giving all the questions, all the answers, and then help you match them up. He will do this by constantly feeding your spirit until you have mastered the subject all the way to the point where you almost without thought or hesitation start to explain the meaning of life and salvation to anyone around you who will listen. This is good because it will help you in your final occupation, in which you are already familiar with because you have been trying to master it your whole life. The job is that of Student/Teacher. You will be the first one to hold this position, so it does not pay very much yet (but we are working on that) but it does have its perks. You make your own schedule, all you have to do is show up for the mid-term and final which should both be easy because as the teacher you will make up all the questions and will be grading the test. And as the only student in the class the only way you could fail would be to show-up put your name and date on the test paper and not answer any of questions. As the teacher you would have to give yourself a zero because even if there was only one question and you graded on a curve your grade would still be zero because you were the only student. As the teacher the only way you could pass yourself would be to write the answer down for your student and you could not do that because that would be cheating. And since the test was left blank as the teacher you must assume the student did not know the answer. So, in shear and utter frustration he up quit for he could never cheat even for himself it would not be fair. "I don't believe this, only God could ruin the perfect job. He arrived at work, clocked in, completed no assignments and for that He would be paid exactly what He had earned- "nothing." But it was His own fault for He would have gotten paid anyway except He forgot to clock out. But that was not really His fault either because He checked his schedule and much to His surprise it was His day off; embarrassed He quickly left without remembering to clock out. So, the only question that remains is: Why didn't He just answer the damn question? For those of you who just asked the stupidest question in the world. I give you this: it is not stupid for the reason you might think. The question was already asked and answered. Do not question Me again for this will make Me truly angry and I am already mad as hell! You have been warned for ignorance will never be an excuse! What was the question? For those of you who just ask this question I suggest that you go back and read this story over again from the beginning. **"WHAT IS GOD'S SALVATION?"** That is my final answer. "Thank You, GERALD for you are the only one who never questioned Me. I owe you big time, I will be forever grateful" **GOD!**

BY: GERALD G. FRIERSON

"And Then There Was One"

And then there was one and that one had to be God. God did not just create the universe He was the universe. Science teaches us that the universe is made up of all energy that can neither be created nor destroyed. God is a Spirit who is made up of 100% pure positive energy. With this energy the Lord created the Heavens and Earth. He also, with this energy, created Adam & Eve- His first born. Why didn't God make Adam & Eve perfect? Why did He put the tree of wisdom in the garden of Eden? First, God did not want to take responsibility for their lives away from them. Secondly, God does not cheat, it would not be fair to anyone, including Himself. And finally, the forbidden fruit represented Adam & Eve's sacrifice and the Lord knew better than anyone that life without sacrifice is barren. (no one is exempt not even God) Just like Adam & Eve the Lord did not want us to be perfect just "imperfectly imperfect." To that end, I have divided the "human being" into five distinct parts. 1) **The Body** – the part of us that needs to eat, drink, and have a need for shelter to stay warm or cool. And finally, a need to procreate and stay healthy. 2) **The Mind** – the part of us that allows us to be rational or to think. This part gives us the ability to learn to and adapt to different situations and environments. 3) **The Heart** – the part of us that allows us to love persons, places, or things. This brings about the desire to communicate. It also, brings about a need to have compassion for others and their property or lack thereof. 4) **The Soul** – this is the part of us that really separates us from everyone else (along with your Spirit). This is where your likes and dislikes are determined, your strengths and weaknesses, and your sense of right and wrong are determined. 5) **The Spirit** – the part of us that God gives each one of us at birth, but no one teaches how to use it. The Spirit is Gods way of feeding us information. The Spirit teaches us the right approach and/or direction to use in all situations; and it will never lead you wrong. Also, the Spirit helps to strengthen and balance out the other four parts of the "human being." This is especially important because any can take the lead in any given situation. And the universe usually attacks your weakest link. And remember the "whole" is always greater than the sum of its parts. That means we should concentrate or focus on the "whole person" rather than the sum of the five parts as listed above. We should take a balanced approach in order to create the best "whole person" we can be. God created us with positive energy; and whenever you create something with positive energy there will always be the creation of negative energy (or waste). This means that we all are made up of a little negative energy. This negative energy can destroy or weaken us if we allow it too. We can prevent this by, first, making ourselves aware of the negative energy inside us; and then concentrate or focus on the positive energy inside us. This approach will lead to a far greater amount of successes in life by creating the "whole person." The approach in the sport of bowling works much the same way. The approach is the area from where you start to the foul line. The approach is the foundation of any consistent good bowler›s game. Most bowlers use either a five or four step approach, but I have seen people use anywhere from a no step to about a ten-step approach with varying degrees of success. Everybody's approach is at least slightly different so start with the basics and do what works best for you and try to be consistent. Anyone can get a strike but if your approach is consistent chances are you will have much more success.

Success in life works pretty much the same way; just take a good consistent approach, for you, and chances are you will have much more success. Life teaches us that we have many choices or no choice at all, depending on the circumstances. How we do in life depends on how well we navigate these choices and circumstances. To this end, I have divided these choices and circumstances into three distinct categories of outcomes. The Good, the Bad, and in the Middle; or positive, negative, and neutral; or positive energy, negative energy, and neutral energy. The Good is a decision or circumstance that has worked well for most of the people in your situation or situation you would like to be in (positive outcome). The Bad is a decision or circumstance that has not worked out well for most of the people in your situation or situation you would like to be in (negative outcome). The Middle is the position you want to be in- this is the "teacher" position. The "teacher" can be both positive and negative depending on what the situation calls for. They can also teach the negative to be more positive and the positive to be more negative when the situation calls for it. Or help the Good and the Bad become neutral or "teachers" as it were. Everyone can teach everyone else something, it is just that no one either listens or listens to the wrong people. Just locate and listen to your "teachers" and you should turn out fine. And remember we must learn to make sacrifices so that our lives will bear fruit. None of us are created perfect and we all make mistakes. Just ask God for forgiveness and He will accept you anyway if you accept Him first. All He expects from you is for you to be "imperfectly imperfect." If you are reading this paper "Victory" is yours, all you must do is claim it! Life was always meant to be challenging but yet not difficult. You just have to "work" your way through it.

BY

GERALD G. FRIERSON

YES, GOD IS HUMAN TOO!

We all know that God is a Spirit, but part of Him had to be human. God created us so He must know something about being a human being. God created Adam in his own image and must have known what he was going to be like. He gave him the ability to think and reason, and the ability to create life and to destroy life. These are the same abilities God has. But He made Adam completely independent of Himself. So, clearly, part of Gods Spirit has to be human. Thank God that He was so generous with these human gifts because He did not have too. In addition, God is not an orphan. God created His parents when He created Father Time and Mother Nature so He would not be alone. No human being would want to be an orphan either (that was not His intention). Let us not forget God is a father too so He knows what it is like to lose a son. God the Father was undoubtedly upset when Jesus was killed on the cross. As a Father, God never got to see his son live out his life. He never got to see His son get married and have kids; just like any father would. That is right God wanted grandkids too! After Jesus rose from the dead God took him up to be with Him. God still wanted grandkids, so He married Jesus to the Holy Spirit. Their first-born son would inherit the world. Who would this be? This could be anyone. The first person to wait on the Lord unconditionally. The first person to not question that God knew what He was doing. The first person to accomplish this was Jesus. It only makes sense that the next person to accomplish this would be the son of Jesus. Everyone knows what the rules are, yet no one has been able to follow them (and ignorance is no excuse). But let us get it straight, Jesus is, and all ways will be the only one to ever live and die perfect. His son would only be a substitute. Let us imagine for a second that the world was turned to nothing. That is right the world ended. The sun exploded and hit the earth. Every nuclear weapon in the world was fired and exploded. There would be nothing left. Nothing! No more people or animals. No more sun or moon- no more light. No more planets or stars. No Heaven or Hell. Nothing to rebuild with not even air to breath. All that would be left is nothing and that nothing would be GOD. So, if you believe in nothing you now believe in GOD too. Because the nothing would be GOD. If you made no investment in GOD, He would give you nothing as a return on your investment; because He is the only one who can bring you back. So clearly, we need GOD more than He needs us. We should invest in Jesus today so that GOD will invest in us later. We do not know when it is going to end so prepare yourself today. You should start praying this very second. Invest a little in GOD and He will invest a lot more in you. That right there is what you call priceless. We call this "Eternal Life."

BY: GERALD G. FRIERSON

THE RULES

GOD gives everyone of us a Human Spirit at birth (not conception) before then you still belong to your mother and father together and will share their fate. I know this may upset some people so let me explain further, if a baby is conceived in a legitimate marriage (and this will be determined by God because He is the only one who can truly marry you.) and that mother was saved before she dies He will replace that baby back in the mother's womb at whatever point it died. But if a woman who died in Christ does not want that baby replaced or could not conceive a baby but desired one, He will fill that void with Himself. Furthermore, anyone who dies in Christ and never married and had no kids they would still be allowed to but only to the same group after Judgment Day. (When this will be no one does not even God, but we do know it will be sooner rather than later but- for all we know it may have already occurred for some people.) And finally, for those of you who come to Christ and have children out of wedlock you must first, get married to someone in Christ if you have not already done so. (or at least get them to come to Christ after marriage for if they don't they will not be allowed into the Kingdom of Heaven with you but you and your children will.) and start a family for God would never break-up a family in Christ. Even if you have unsaved children in your household (under 18) because God will take care of that problem for you even if you have given up. OK, now we must deal with God's favorites, the group of men and women (over 18) who have come to Christ and do not want to get married and/or have children and have no desire to do either. You will be considered to be married to the Church and will be helping God take care of the saved and unsaved children, the elderly and the sick, and in general anyone who is saved and cannot take care of themselves and that includes the handicapped no matter what that handicap might be. And yes, even gays and lesbians who have received Christ in their lives will be welcomed in God's Church as long as they are married (to be confirmed by God only). He may never understand it himself but realizes that if they are truly gay or lesbian (they were born that way) then that was his mistake and as we all know God makes no mistakes so, they must, by rule, be allowed into heaven as well. But if they are not truly gay or lesbian then they are sick and if that is the case God will heal them Himself. In other word, God will deal with this matter Himself because discrimination of any kind will not be tolerated in God's House. And <u>all</u> who cannot live with that will be evicted and sent straight to HELL and in all these matters God will always be both judge and jury, but as always, He will go out of his way to be fair. Note: in this paper (so I do not have to keep repeating myself) anytime it is said something will not be tolerated; eviction and sent straight to HELL is what that means.

BY: GERALD G. FRIERSON

THE RULES OF ENGAGEMENT

THE RULES(PART II)

First of all, no one will be allowed to marry before they turn 18 and have achieved a high school diploma or GED. And for any adults who don't have a high school diploma or GED they must be given, as a right, an opportunity to go back and get one, no matter what their age but only if they so choose. But let me make one thing clear, to those of you who are under 18 (not yet adults); unless you have a disability or handicap that prevents it high school drop-outs will not be tolerated. Education is much to important. Education, much like life, should be challenging but yet not difficult. So parents you should pay more attention to the behavior and work habits grades for unless your child is handicapped; if your child is paying attention and is willing to do the work the subject grade should take care of itself. But if it does not it either means the teacher, the school, or the subject was not meant for your child. Or just maybe it was you who is not paying attention and have poor work habits for it is you who are your child's first teacher. In any case, this cannot, should not and will not be tolerated. Yes, God can and will hold you accountable for your child; so take the problem to God and He will either teach your child Himself or He will find your child a suitable tutor but don't let the problem be you because that will not be tolerated. Fornication will never be tolerated for we must all learn to wait. Oral and annal sex, is real sex, and will not be tolerated unless you are married and it is performed with the expressed mutual consent of both parties to the one marriage. But either and or both partners to the one marriage may revoke their consent at any and all times, and this must be respected by both partners for under any other circumstances it will not be tolerated. Adultery will never be tolerated and that includes annal and oral sex. Kissing, hugging, flirting, handshakes, and touching- none of these acts are in and of itself, should not be considered adultery and GOD will not grant you a divorce because of them. But these acts can be very disrespectful to your partner. You should, first, admit that you do them and to what extent and discuss with your partner what acts they would consider disrespectful. (and don't forget

The Meaning of Life

to discuss how the rules might change when your partner is not around). Notice I did not use the word spouse for these rules apply to to single couples in committed relationship too. Being disrespectful is not necessarily a sin but being disobedient to GODS word is and will not be tolerated. This must apply to all our relationships but in some relationships respect must be given but in others it must be earned. So try not to be disrespectful in all your relationships because GOD does have his limits but HE will always be fair so we should be fair in our relationships too! In other words, disrespect will sometimes be tolerated in some relationships but never tolerated in others. Ex: GOD said we should honor our mother and father. But some rules were meant to be broken but you must earn HIS respect in order to break them. GOD will never blame the victim, HIS kids (Adam&Eve) taught HIM that, because through them HE learned HE was a victim too! So if and when you ever feel disrespected in any of your relationships you must always speak-up. For no one is a mind reader nor does anyone want to be a victim just ask GOD. In other words, if you feel like you need help in or with any of your relationships you must ask for GODS help for HE will never take responsibility for your life a way from you. But always remember this: GODS job one is to serve and protect HIS children. So if you are truly a child of GOD, rest easy, because at this job HE must, can, will never fail. For even if HE needed to take a mental health day off (all true teachers and/or parents get them you know; not to be confused with sick days because as we all know GOD can never get sick) you can still feel safe because you know HE is always on call, all you have to do is call HIS name. Also, incest, child abuse of any kind, any and all forms of rape (and date rape will always be rape), and sex with animals will not be tolerated. In addition, any and all forms of unwanted physical body contact (if one or both parties felt disrespected) will not be tolerated. But if neither party indicates any disrespect consent maybe implied (for no one is a mind reader); but this consent maybe revoked at any and all times and must be respected by both parties. For any and all of the above behaviors will not be tolerated under any other circumstances. The right to add, alter, or change any of the above rules or language thereof will be held solely by GOD. This is good.

Yours Truly,
THE CREATOR

by
GERALD G. FRIERSON

ABOUT THE AUTHOR/BOOK

Gerald G. Frierson has a Bachelor of Arts degree in criminal justice from Temple University. He also, graduated from the PJA paralegal school. It is during this education that he developed his unique and clever writing style. This is a life's work for Mr. Frierson and his first book. Also, Mr. Frierson has started his own Life Coaching Company which is based largely on the book and is called G FRIERSON MARKETING INC.

Life teaches us that we have many choices or no choice at all. We can choose to believe in GOD or not to believe in GOD. You can choose to believe in yourself or not to believe in yourself. You can believe in something or you can believe in nothing. But we should always choose life over death. If life has no meaning, then there is really no reason to live.

We should always try and live life to the fullest. GOD is the reason why we live but how we live is totally up to us. "THE MEANING OF LIFE" is a true story, and not necessarily because it is true but because of what it teaches you about life. Life's about choices and what this book does is help you to make the right choices for you, good or bad, right or wrong. Ultimately, you will have to make and take responsibility for your own decisions in life. What this book does is help you navigate your way through your choices and through life. And remember your decisions not only affect you but everyone around you. How can you truly be happy if everyone around you is unhappy? The ultimate goal of "THE MEANING OF LIFE" is to help everyone who reads it discover his or her purpose in life. Congratulations! You have just discovered "THE MEANING OF LIFE" now please tell all your friends and loved ones. "Thank You" and Enjoy!

www.ingramcontent.com/pod-product-compliance
Lightning Source LLC
Chambersburg PA
CBHW020549080526
44583CB00013B/1064